Intimate Power
Autobiography of a City

CATHERINE MORRIS

SPRING PUBLICATIONS

THOMPSON, CONN.

Published by Spring Publications,
Thompson, Conn.
www.springpublications.com

First edition 2025 (1.0)

ISBN: 978-0-88214-179-4

Library of Congress Control Number: 2024951493

This book is dedicated
in solidarity to

Médecins Sans Frontières

&

The Domestic Violence Response Unit in Galway

*I really liked and admired this text: its openness at once to
European historical moments and to personal insights, at that point
where the two might merge. The citations and quotations also bring
out the sense in which each of the "historical" quotations was once
an individual history, with the pressure of felt experience, before
becoming a social truth. The I\she bifurcation helped to bring out
the dichotomy but also the hope of some underlying unity knotting
all of these disparate experiences together. The same could be said
of the various parent/child meditations. The images come at exactly
the appropriate moment. The different texts, taken together, seemed
to offer an analysis of the city as a sort of urban-peasant-place—
a point of convergence for modernity, yes, but also a holding-centre
for the multiple experiences of those who fetched up there.*
    —Declan Kiberd, Professor emeritus of Irish Studies,
        Notre Dame University

I read and greatly admired Intimate Power: Autobiography of a City *over
the summer. As I prepared to leave Liverpool after my 22 years there, I'd been
watching Terence Davies (what a loss) and revisiting Jeff Young (Ghost Town
remains magnificent)—and this book belongs squarely to that rare corpus of
such subtle, spectral evocations of the city and the fragmented layers of which it
consists. What Catherine Morris is doing is rather different, of course, with the
entangling of the city into those broader international, even global histories and
geographies. Morris captures the soundscapes, with their multilingual echoes,
so beautifully also, and I was of course delighted that the author reveals traces
of Frenchness, actual and imagined, that surround us, not least the Lumieres'
travelling shots . . . The sense of place Morris triggers through her walking is
so well-observed, but I was struck by the way these microjourneys are never
introverted, always relational and open to elsewhere: Charles Wootton linked
to the FLN supporters drowned in Paris in October 1961; the Mujeres Libres
recalling the Communardes; and all the fleeting travel stories to which the author
alludes to throughout, not least of the runaway from Prescot (those telegraphic ads
are so moving), of the boys in the workhouse on Brownlow Hill (what happened
to Higgins who "escaped over the wall"?), of the Shanghai seamen treated so
shamefully in 1946, of the famine refugees, and of those children deported to*

CONTENTS

BROKEN THREADS

Home is a place in the mind. When it is empty it
frets. It is fretful with memory, faces and places
and times gone by . . . the long gaze back is always
turned inward.

— Maeve Brennan, *The Visitor* (1940)

On Salisbury Dock, six clocks on the Victoria Tower navigated
emotional liminality between two river gates: nine-year-old
Michael Higgins was one of the 300,000 Irish Famine refugees
who arrived onto the River Mersey in 1847 as the tower's bell
sounded out warnings of fog and imminent changes to the
tides. After the President of Ireland, Michael D. Higgins, asked
to see the Liverpool-Irish archives that I had uncovered while
researching this book, we stood together in Central Library and
read as his namesake leaped out of the panopticon of Brownlow
Hill Workhouse and into history: "Michael Higgins: escaped
over the wall." Arrivals and return journeys; escape routes out
of coercive institutions that remain open when collectively felt.
Gazing at the Berlin Wall an angel in Wim Wenders's film *Wings
of Desire* whispers: "I want to transmute. To sustain a glance."
Transformations in narrative; a constellation of fragments that
together tell a different story. A 1907 newspaper report documented
how Mary Quinn in Omagh "escaped from the laundry on the
evening of 15th December but was not missed till bedtime . . . she

escaped again on the 24th." A glimpse of stolen freedom breathed in the long-ago of a Christmas Eve. After the Berlin Wall fell in 1989, I lay alone in a maternity ward in Liverpool while *The Irish Times* reported how people performed acts of freedom that hours earlier would have resulted in death: "An elderly man strode back and forth on numerous occasions across a white line which separated East from West. On the bridge, a woman raced forward good-humouredly towards the crossing as if trying to escape."[1]

While *Intimate Power: Autobiography of a City* is a meditation on the personal losses that we carry with us all our lives it simultaneously serves as a recovery of voice for the kinds of trauma that the city has carried through successive generations be it slavery, famine, war, asylum or exile. The book is a series of walks through Liverpool made on a return journey from a feeling of long exile. It is a recovery of voice through which I situate parts of my own life into a collective solidarity that I sought out in conversations, chance encounters and in the stories that I uncovered in the city's local and international multimedia archives. I walk through versions of myself in Liverpool via twenty episodes that I name after revolutions: moments in which transformations occur. Each revolution is connected through inter-episodes of "Walking" that carry the words of the living and of the dead.

I began to make a new archive of my micro-journeys during the lead up to, and in the immediate aftermath of, the 2016 Referendum to leave the European Union. Liverpool felt to me then like a series of thresholds; as though to hear myself think about the broken threads in my own life was to cross over into a city making and unmaking itself across time. In filming his autobiographical movie *Roma* in 2018, Alfonso Cuarón made his own return journey to the Mexico of 1971 by intensive acts of verisimilitude and remembering that were collective and live: new memories were evoked for the director and his cast as they witnessed the fragments of a known narrative play out again in the streets and buildings of the reconstructed cinematic city of his

birth: "Our perception of space lingers longer than time itself," he
observed. "Time immediately fades away."[2]

Herman Melville arriving as a sailor in the 1840s used his
father's map of Liverpool to navigate the city and the self:
"when he walked this flagging I was not so much as thought of;
I was not included in the census of the universe. My own father did
not know me then."[3] I walked the city without a map and instead
followed the pattern of memory and chance encounter towards
conversation wherever possible. I ventured into grand buildings that
were once the economic laundry of Empire and that remain to this
day like film sets vacated after the story has moved on: bank vaults
that had once held the world's gold were being flooded into spas,
shipping insurance headquarters vacated to make way for hotels,
tobacco warehouses remade into apartments.

Liverpool time-travels through the imaginary as its buildings
and streets morph into an on-screen body-double performing
other countries, cities and times: I watch as snow falls in Summer;
yesterday on my way to the library, St George's Hall was being
Moscow; a deserted road in the Welsh Streets translates in time to
become the blacked-out Birmingham headquarters of 1920s crime
gang the Peaky Blinders. As swifts flew into Sefton Park from
south Sahara and butterflies arrived from the mountains of Central
Mexico, I watched days in Liverpool play out in the Northern
Film Archive. I photographed moments of the city captured in old
film reels; researched what was in the newspaper that a man was
reading in front of the Adelphi Hotel as a tram passes him in 1919
with a camera mounted to its top deck: the Paris Peace Conference.
Jacques Derrida in *Right of Inspection* reflects: "You should speak of
these photographs as of a thinking, as a pensiveness without voice,
whose only voice remains suspended."[4]

After being invited to become Liverpool Central Library's
first ever Writer-in-Residence, I connected my autobiographical
enquiry with a utopian space that stores and enables shared memory
in the city: war records, ships' passenger logs, maps, newspapers,

photographs, parish registers of births, deaths, marriages, orphanage and workhouse records, diaries, letters, political campaign archives, census documentation. In situating my attempt to find voice in the city of my birth, I also talked with those who were trying to make sense of their own stories as they searched for European roots, the unmarked graves of children, African DNA. My ancestors (Learys from Wexford, Mary Quinn from County Tyrone, a shoemaker from Clonmel, a great grandmother from Sligo) find their own voices in this narrative. In the lead up to Brexit, I heard people describe unexpected discoveries: one woman, whose family name was Spanish, on receiving a copy of her birth certificate was forced to ask her father, "when were you going to tell me I was adopted?"

What does it feel like to return to a place that is no longer *home*? When Edward Said was eventually allowed to return to his childhood home, he chose not to enter the building. Standing instead on the street outside of the house in 1998 he told his son: "My connection with Palestine is always intellectual and cultural and, in some sense, spiritual but not physical. And I've resigned myself to the loss of this place [he points to his childhood home], but I still feel a moral commitment to it because I think it is terribly unjust and the injustice done to us has never really been acknowledged."[5] Fragments and ruins are the architecture of my own sense of the past. Like Maeve Brennan, I found myself "looking for the voice in which I can say anything in." Living out the last decade of his life in an Italian prison cell, Marxist philosopher Antonio Gramsci wrote often about broken threads: "every day I seem to feel less desire to write letters. It is as if, every day, another thread tying me to the past breaks, and it becomes ever more impossible to knot these threads together again."[6] Departures and losses: broken threads of my own life are like fragments when fragments are an articulation of trauma. Olga Tokarczuk in her 2018 Nobel speech urges us to trust in fragments: "as it is fragments that create constellations capable of describing more, and in a more complex way, multi-dimensionally."[7]

During the rise of fascism that would consign Gramsci to prison, German Jewish writer Walter Benjamin excavated his own memories from a precarious exile that would end in suicide somewhere along the border between France and Spain. Realizing he would never see Berlin again, Benjamin's prose fragments read like an X-ray: "These childhood memories" he explained, "are not narratives in the form of a chronicle but . . . individual expeditions into the depths of memory."[8] *Intimate Power* documents the arrivals and the departures of people whose voices I recovered in the archives as I searched for a way out of the silences of institutionalized shame and into a collective reanimation of local and international connection. A journalist in the 1840s witnessed a female refugee in Liverpool screaming as though already silenced: "What will I do without my tongue?" Looking back into her own life, French philosopher and novelist Simone de Beauvoir asked: "What has it meant to me to be a woman?"[9] I ask this question in narrative fragments that together articulate coercions girls and women encounter when forced into situations made to limit the dimensions of their lives, bodies, imaginations and voicess.

Agnès Varda's 1962 French New Wave film *Cléo from 5 to 7* depicts a woman who walks the city while waiting for cancer test results. Although Cléo is a fictional character, Varda constructs her journey through Paris using documentary techniques of filmmaking: "We chose not to cheat with the distance of geography."[10] The camera stays on Cléo as she takes each step and captures how people watch her from doorways as she makes her way through the emotional range of her waiting. Subjective and objective time merge in the urban textures of cafes, weather, cars, pedestrians, shop windows, advertisements and street performers. As Cléo encounters herself in mirrored reflections of Paris, the city breathes the day out in real time. Varda's feminist lens shakes the central character's viewpoint out of relentless interiority and into a sense of contextualized agency that is socially located: "She becomes a woman who sees. She's no longer seen . . . she sees."

After the last Magdalene Laundry closed in 1996 and the last Mother and Baby home closed in 1998, a series of reports began to reveal the extent of violence and coercion endemic within these institutions and across social attitudes. In 2021, the *Taoiseach* broadcast a public apology for the way women who had given birth out of wedlock had been shamed and stigmatized. Home is a place in the mind. Maya Angelou believed that "the 'I' is a universal 'we'. The 'I' should be the third person plural . . ." she explained, because "facts can obscure the truth, what it really felt like."[11] While the fragmented narrative perspective of this book is constantly moving, the I/she/her is stilled in that long gaze back. *I want to transmute. To sustain a glance.* Documenting her own feminist navigations towards the self, poet Adrienne Rich concluded: "I need to understand how the place on the map is also a place in history within which . . . I am created and trying to create. Begin, though, not with a continent or a country or a house, but with the geography closest in—the body. Here at least I know I exist, that living human individual whom the young Marx called 'the first premise of all human history.' "[12]

NOTES

1. *The Irish Times,* 11 November 1989.

2. Alfonso Cuarón in *The Road to Roma,* directed by Andres Clariond and Gabriel Nuncio (Netflix Studios, 2020).

3. *Redburn,* in *The Works of Herman Melville,* vol. 5 (London, Bombay, and Sydney: Constable and Company, 1922), 196.

4. Jacques Derrida, *Right of Inspection,* translated by David Wills; photographs by Marie-Françoise Plissart (New York: The Monacelli Press, 1998), n.p.

5. *In Search of Palestine: Edward Said's Return Home,* BBC documentary, 1998.

6. Antonio Gramsci, *Letters from Prison,* selected, translated from the Italian, and introduced by Lynne Lawner (New York: Harper & Row, 1973), 201 n.2

7. Olga Tokarczuk, "The Tender Narrator," Nobel Lecture in Literature, December 7, 2018, Swedish Academy, Stockholm; online at *https://www.nobelprize. org/prizes/literature/2018/tokarczuk/lecture/*

8. Walter Benjamin, B*erlin Childhood around 1900,* translated by Howard Eiland (Cambridge, Mass., and London: The Belknap Press of Harvard University Press, 2006), xii.

9. Simone de Beauvoir, *Force of Circumstance,* translated by Richard Howard (New York: G. P. Putnam's Sons, 1965), 94.

10. Agnès Varda speaking about the making of *Cléo from 5 to 7* in *Varda by Agnès,* directed by Didier Rouget and Agnès Varda (Ciné-Tamaris/ARTE, 2019).

11. Maya Angelou with George Plimpton, January 11, 1988, 92Y/ The Paris Review Interview Series (online at *https://youtu.be/XYn3HFg_ T0o?si=VeIGymNwQVQXL1jK*).

12. Adrienne Rich, *Blood, Bread, and Poetry: Selected Prose 1979–1985* (New York and London: W.W. Norton & Company, 1986), 212.

1

1789: THE FRENCH REVOLUTION

The door that I was closing opened. It was forced open from the outside. I didn't recognize the made-up face in a mirror. A breach of self-privacy; maybe that is what memory is—if we return too far, we breach a wall, a door, enter into a private space that was never . . .

An elephant walked down County Road. Sounds of Yiddish caught somewhere between doorways, she could hear the world of the city spoken by her Russian grandmother. Brenda said: "A sudden feeling of fate attached itself to my life as I sat in the small hospital room nursing a child recently arrived from Jamaica." 1949. "Windrush"— a word that has been mentioned before.

High up above Liverpool—or on the prow of a ship
vertigo making her fall.
Her father paused in reaching to steady her
—he got his pencil and made a mark on the indented triangular
stepped shape that was a compass or the center
—that pencil, him making that small mark—that was as much his
identity as a line of destiny on his hand.

Walking to the hospital to see her father, people stood motionless and silent; a net of poppies cast out over the granite pillars of St George's Hall. She realized she was standing at the exact spot the Lumière Brothers had placed their camera in 1896, staring into the face of a boy breathing in the amber of celluloid. A child stands for a split second in the middle of the road, his jacket pinned together. He places his left hand above his eyes—to shade his gaze from direct sunlight, his right hand beneath his chin framing his face to the choreography of memory. He walks towards the camera and enters into the future in which he will be blown to pieces on the Somme or in the Dublin Post Office. Liverpool holds his glance forever. *What does forever mean?*

She had gone into the library on that Tuesday afternoon in November to find out where I was; to discover where I had been born—Who were my parents? Who were my grandparents? she asked. "Do you have parents?" I replied.

Even when someone does not die in attempting suicide—a kind of death takes place, she thought as she walked up London Road towards the hospital.

Famine
Spanish Civil War
The dock lock out
All the voices and struggles that have passed through this city. The 'death house' on the Docks, fever sheds on the Mersey, Famine cages where suicides can be seen and claimed; seen and forgotten . . .
Walter Benjamin said: "these childhood memories are . . . not narratives in the form of a chronicle but . . . individual expeditions into the depths of memory."
All the voices, all the lives.

Amber reflecting, coloring the darkness of the cobbles along Faulkner Square, Catharine Street, Back Canning Street. I walk along Granby Street and later take a left at the Florrie. In the absolute darkness of half lit roads where houses are boarded up, I find myself back where I began yesterday. The darkness is more than anything I have encountered. "Demolish"—is this an order?

A threat? A fact? These terraced rows become past tense. I stand in the blackout.

At The Empress, a man plays darts: the ghost of Ringo waving down from windows now bricked up. A woman in a dressing gown comes out of his house and goes next door-but-three to a house where the door remains open. "Whatareya lookin' foooor?" she asks impatiently as I walk past the doorway of the living room that is also the hallway. She speaks into the house and not at me—but I, like the person who replies, do not know what I am looking for. A hair brush, a purse, keys, glasses, phone, happiness, an income, the traces of a stolen child. Anything and anyone who might give me permission to know that I have already arrived. So close are the doorways that formal clothes are not felt necessary in the momentary transitions from home to home. Public space disappears; worn to an intimate groove. But that community felt a little exposed tonight shrouded in black-out darkness of so many evictions. Hard to see even at a short distance. Was it easy to forget the families and voices; the dressing gowns and familiarity that once meant so much to a musician that his local, The Empress, made the cover of his first solo album?

At the wake for the EU in Liverpool everyone drank but nobody got drunk. The instruments were out but nobody played—just the slow Mexican Irish Italian sea shanty sounded somewhere. A funeral procession walking through the streets of a Spanish village, along past an Italian Square where so much was understood and forgotten in the telling. We talked a little about Wittgenstein and that cottage he stayed in on the hill side of Ireland's only Fjord. "He had had a break-down and so followed his psychiatrist over from Cambridge to Dublin," Luke said. I follow his footsteps as he leaves the Aisling Hotel tracing his way along Wolfe Tone Quay crossing O'Malin Bridge to Heuston Station. Boarding the train West, I arrive at Killary Harbor and wait in Gaynor's Bar. The storm had not yet broken Leenane Bridge—a crossing we thought could never fall. On the edge of the boat you make a pact with me: 'if anything should happen to us can we leave her in your care.' My second daughter. We read the will and travel further out passing Oscar Wilde's father. Wittgenstein's boat.

I make my way back along the Famine Road. Past the still hidden Hedge School on my way through Connemara. I board the boat back to Liverpool and watch them travel. Moving. Arriving. Writing their journey out in letters home. The ink still wet—a half remembered moment when home was still home. Marriages, births. 'Cigar maker,' 'Weaver,' 'Hawker.' Washing children. Cooking food every day for seventy seven years on the same stove. "I couldn't even speak to my mother. Voted out," the gallery worker said. Her colleague behind the desk answered: "Yeah, I haven't spoken to my da for days." My dad said in a broken slow quiet almost voice: "It's last what happened girl. Absolutely last." Aged 87, he had voted Remain. "We're going to elope," said the married daughter as though to run off with your husband to another land was an act of re-marriage or protest. An artist who had arrived at the Bluecoat Arts Centre from Jamaica that day was asked a question about the connections between Bristol, Liverpool, and the Caribbean: "Will this be a part of your work here?" "I don't know," he answered. "I don't know where I am yet." None of us know where we are now.

On Faulkner Square Barry said:
They class all of us as African Caribbean you know. Liverpool.
It could do better. No matter
where you come from we are all one people.

On Shaw Street Bettie said:
To say my mother worked so hard—she lived till she was 92.
Never went to school; her mother had too many children,
she used to be there for these babies—had no time for school.

In the Toxteth library the newspaper journalist recorded:
The worst night of bombing was Saturday, May 3 into Sunday, May 4,
when enemy aircraft dropped around 363 tonnes of high explosives
and 50,000 incendiary bombs on Liverpool.

On Derby Square Churchill said:
I see the damage done by the enemy attacks
but I also see the spirit of an unconquered people.

In the porch of the Royal Academy Bill Nighy said:
My days at the Everyman were the best days.

On the corner of Shaw Street Stephen said:
Just here there was what you call "The Parish"
what you call today the Dole. . .
it was a bad place.

On Gerard Street Petra said:
If you've got a house to keep and three children to keep
and you can't always go out or the weather stopped you—
you had to get money and what you went through
to get that few shillings . . .

2

1791: SAINT-DOMINGUE SLAVE REVOLT

Who was it that the police were drowning in the Seine in the early 1960s? I think of Charles Wotton here. 1919. A Bermudan sailor, home from War, pelted to death with stones as he drowned in the River Mersey.

"I've worked here for 29 years. When work dried up for me on the docks I got a job as a cleaner here. Worked my way up." He stands and collects tickets of all the travelers passing through the barriers at Lime Street.

1919. A cinecamera fixed to the front of a tram records how the city moves like a dream through winter. A man reads his newspaper in a warm overcoat as he waits outside the Adelphi. 1919. The cotton is on fire at the docks. St Luke's clock still ticks. 1919. Not yet Civil War in Ireland. What was in that newspaper that he reads? So busy he cannot look up at the tram that has stopped and the tram that is a second away.

Ghosts of the enslaved; their mark of absence arriving on ships that passed in and out of the Mersey. Those who built and owned slave ships here in Liverpool. Those who built and owned plantations far away. Interconnected distances. Which United Irishman in 1798 said: "In every spoon of sugar, I see a drop of blood"?

The waterfront.
The East Africa Bank.

The East India Insurance Company.
The Royal Insurance Company.
Cafes and sweet shops now. To let. To let. To let.

I know they are here. Deep within a village of their lives. Like
living in the middle of a deep forest. I know they are here in this
city. They are here. Tonight.

Outside under a streetlight she looked into a map of the disappeared.
Ghost streets. Conway, Luther, Ellison, Elias, Robesart, Beatrice,
Opie, Arkright, Kew, Benledi, William Moult, Taliesin, Juvenal,
Dryden, Virgil, Rachel, Beau, Aughton, Mitylene, Conyers, Zante.
Scattered lives; collected in the aftermath of clearances.

No trace of why everything is the way it is. No trace of all the work
that people did. No trace of the sounds and the movement and the
early mornings and dark late nights. No crates, no ropes, no ships,
no boats, no men, no women workers. No great journeys in or out.
No farewell scenes. No imaginations looking beyond. No fears or
hopes. No steps to climb out from the city and into another life.
No looking back and seeing all that was familiar disappear. No
sacks of sugar or oats or coffee. No storage. No horses. No electric
rail line. No trams. No arrivals. No pen and pencil to document
and sign you in. No journeys beginning here. No Michael Quinn
arriving to seek out his sister. No letters home to New York,
Somalia, Angola, Ethiopia, or Ireland. No music coming in on the
boats as through a transistor radio. No boats. No ships. No people
passing. Oh my daughter. I look at the River. See all the way into
the distance of empty water. Where are the trains to evacuate my
parents in their seven year old selves? Deep in a village of their own
lives, their own people. They own. They belong. Theirs. What is
mine? I recognize bus numbers. I know street names and how one
road leads into another.

On Apollo Street Abeba said:
I've been in the queue in the pawn shop many times.
Kids would
stand in that queue.

On Pitt Street Roscoe said:
The abuse poured out against me was unbounded.
I am represented as an enemy to the King,
and as having taken bread out of the mouths of the people
of Liverpool by abolishing the Slave Trade.

On Nelson Street Louam said:
We came out of the shelter into the
back yard and this fire bomb was blazing away . . .

On Lawrence Street Hideaki said:
Everything comes into the city from the river.
Whereas years ago you used to get a lot of seafarers,
I get the atmosphere of the city now as not being real.

On Tabley Street Mick said:
Your working week was based on a 56-hour working week . . .
every clock had a different time on it . . .
You spend a lot of time on the river—
dodging the tides or just
waiting for whatever times the ships are coming in.

On Circus Street Eric said:
The cinemas in Italy were requisitioned by the army . . .
the Piazza Bar Marini . . . a single screen cinema with a sliding roof
so you could sit in the middle of the summer
and you could see the stars and watch the film . . .

LIVERPOOL UNEMPLOYED MARCH LONDON

3

1798: UNITED IRISH REVOLUTION

In 1971, an antiques dealer was called in to a house on Shaw Street to assess furniture with a view to possibly purchasing. "The smell, the atmosphere. It was very strange and I've been in some weird places. In the cellar I saw ropes for people to rent and rest their heads on while they slept."

In a military witness statement Frank Thornton remembered: "We boarded the 'St. Paul' at Princes Landing Stage on that day and carried O'Donovan's remains right along the Dock Road, the journey being over two miles. I think it can safely be claimed that by this method O'Donovan Rossa's body had landed in Ireland when we took him on our Irish shoulders at Prince's Landing Stage.

At Dove Cottage Dorothy Wordsworth wrote: "a sailor who was traveling from Liverpool called; he was faint and pale when he knocked at the door... His name was Isaac Chapel. He had been at sea since he was 15 years old. He was by trade a sail maker. His last voyage was to the coast of Guinea. He had been on board a slave ship, the Captain's name Maxwell, where one man had been killed, a boy put to lodge with the pigs and was half eaten, one boy set to watch in the hot sun till he dropped down dead... He was exceedingly like my brother John."

Up and out along the coffin road for the papers, the post. I climb higher, level the pattern of snow that caps the northern facing peaks.

Father Abdoulaye got in his car at the Sailor's Home to go and collect a sailor stranded in the city center by Debenhams: "They have four hours and they want to do everything: they want to go to the Beatles Museum, see Anfield, Abbey Road, then shop at Asda and Argos."

At the Casa Community Centre on Hope Street, Tony said: "The port of Liverpool—what is it and what will it become? The bigger the ships, the further up from the city the dock moves."

Brownlow Hill, Mount Pleasant, Mount Zion, Hope Street, Rodney Street, Canning Street, Faulkner Square, Percy Street. The sun shines on Liverpool today. The Shelter for Orphaned Children. The Institute for the Blind. The Bluecoat Orphan School. The Institute for Destitute Children. Nazareth House for unmarried women and 'illegitimate' children. The Italian men and women and children rounded up on 29 June 1940; the Chinese seamen forcibly repatriated in 1946: they shade their eyes from the heat of this sun. "Feels like a Spanish morning. Or like a Spanish winter's morning perhaps." It is March. Is it International Women's Day today?

Every threshold I pass below, I risk being turned to gold, taken to the cellar vaults and kept. Perhaps everyone who passed through these doors turned to gold. Their assets invested by Martin's Bank transformed magically into stocks, shares.

What did they see from their boardroom? Sugar refineries, tobacco warehouses, Ogden's factory, Notre Dame, the Welsh Cathedral. The last decade before the Empire would finally fall; they looked down into Insurance buildings . . . What do I see now? The Cunard Building. Empty passenger lounges and first-class waiting rooms waiting, waiting, waiting for what? Private oak-paneled telephone booths and no telephones in sight. The old baggage-hold. So far below. Another bunker. Another secret underground. Times of day, shipping forecasts, wooden racks, labels for the Gold Coast,

Zambia, South Africa. A scattered archive of papers left behind by shipping companies long gone.

The vaults are empty of gold. The filing cabinet for 'debts written off' is bare. A steel bar has been welded so that the doors cannot close. The codes for locking the safe forgotten. "They are making it into a five-star hotel. This basement will be made into a spa and a swimming pool." The echo of my footsteps disappears into the waters of swimmers and steam. "I'm here eighteen years. In May they move in. The old tenants now are all moving out. You're probably the last to see it as it is now. I'll know soon if I still have a job." It is March. May is two months away.

"You can't go up there. But look." A security guard takes me down two flights and points: "That's the only original stained-glass window that survived the War." Where was it? Which place in Empire? Rhodesia?

The city rains night. Lights burning time out to the river and across to where the bombs fell. Distances etched into this landscape of relationships like the gaping yields of a quarry. Over there. I know they are not two miles away, my parents. I am stranded still.

The map of WWII looks like the map of the sea. The sky at night. Islands and continents etched in blue chalk. An orange piece of wool the defining line that crosses, translates, makes shape, gives sense to action. A pin with a yellow circle and a red circle defines another action, marks another incident of secret warfare in the black, in the blue. Mannequins perform a history suspended in time; frozen in mid-action they hold ladders, push markers across the sea, type in codes, decipher to communicate. Each locked in a coded cell in the underground network that is Derby Buildings.

On Water Street Alexandros said:
I went to get me passport. You know, because of Brexit.
A copy of my birth certificate arrived.
I called my father: "I'm not Italian, am I?
When were you going to tell me I was adopted?"

On Dublin Street Medbh reading from Joyce's Ulysses said:
Where are the Greek merchants who came through the pillars
of Hercules, the Gibraltar now grabbed . . . with gold
and tyrian purple to sell in Wexford at the fair . . .

On Hope Street Tony said:
I can't see it lasting.
We're getting crushed every day that goes by . . .
I'm just fearful that
The Lock Out . . .
I've got a massive fear that it will be forgotten.
A pathological fear.
Unless somebody keeps telling the story
I'm just fearful . . .
I know it won't be forgotten
but it won't be told by our lads.
That's the problem.
They can't go through it all again.
They feel let down and angry.
Angry when they speak about it . . .
To live on £40 a week is almost impossible.
It took them a while to get on benefits—
the kids —they withstood the hardship

4

1807: ABOLITION OF SLAVERY

Maybe the dislocation between the 'I' and the 'she' is the distance between the river and the city.

Headlines projected at The Futurist Cinema in 1929:

"Eighty per cent of England's cotton imports are financed, warehoused and sold in Liverpool."

"The World's largest warehouse is used for storing tobacco."

"The Cotton 'Futures' market."

"Liverpool brings Fruit from the World's orchards for 15, 000, 000 British appetites."

"A Fruit Exchange auction."

"A cargo can be auctioned and put in the country's shop window on the same day."

"£10, 000,000 worth of Timber enters the Port of Liverpool every year."

"A Timber sale in progress. Some of these Mahogany logs are worth £1, 000 each."

"Cattle and Frozen meat from British Dominions."

"The Gladstone Docks, the largest in the World."

"Dockland from the Overhead Railway."

"Liverpool is still growing."
"Liverpool Cathedral, which, when completed will be twice the size of Westminster Abbey."

"Locomotives leaving Birkenhead for India. Nearly half the Exports of Britain pass through the Port of Liverpool."

I walk down Rodney Street and post the letter. Their ferry journey over to Ireland and back via first-class gold-card out on the Irish sea swirls around my mind. To remember. Perhaps that is enough. Like watching out for Mrs Williams's candle that burned in her window reminding us of her life, each day, each night. "I am not long for this world."

"My father watched the 1911 strike from the steps of the Walker Art Gallery."

Catherine: "What did it feel like to be expelled?"
Tony: "To be expelled? You would need a chapter to itself to describe what that was like. The star chamber. The report that thick," (he shows a large space of air between his finger and his thumb) "to discredit us."

I am sitting on the steps by Central Library reading Franz Fanon *The Wretched of the Earth* wondering if I have the right time and the correct place. He walks across the cobbles wearing a white linen suit and a panama hat. A newspaper under his arm. Cunard Yank, I think, as I see him striding across Brownlow Hill.

'She doesn't want to be found.' I can hear the ancestors saying. Baffled at how I managed to slip through the fence . . .

On Brook Street Philip said:
He'd been refused asylum and he'd been living on the streets
I was typing away trying to get him access to accommodation.
"Look at this picture. This was me."
Small phone; little grainy picture.
"This was the first day I arrived."
It was just him, smiling the best smile ever
a blanket of snow behind him.
"This was the first day I arrived. I had never seen snow."
I'm looking at him
holding this picture:
his face then and the way he is now.
The journey.
It doesn't end when you get to the White Cliffs of Dover.
Not only are you suffering from the persecution
you've escaped from,
you are having to negotiate this opaque system
that feels like it's structured to
beat you down into the dust...
There is that survivors' guilt...
one of the boats had sunk.
"I've lost all my friends."

On Hope Street a son of a Spanish Civil War fighter said:
When I was eleven I went away to sea with him.
We went to France. 1952
The skipper took his lad and he took me.
And when we got to Paris
we met the people who couldn't go back to Spain
they'd got over the Pyrenees
there was a big Spanish community in Paris then.
I'll always remember it.
First time I'd had a Spanish omelet you know...

5

1848: EUROPEAN REVOLUTIONS

Simone de Beauvoir said: "I wanted my blood to circulate in this narrative; I wanted to fling myself into it, still very much alive—to put myself in question before all questions are silenced. Perhaps it is too soon; but tomorrow it certainly will be too late."

When do all these certainties begin to fall apart? When an almost suicide pulls the chain so hard and so unexpectedly that all the links are strained.

On St Oswald Road Sister Carmel said:
Dublin?...I left it behind.
You were allowed to write just once a month,
that was your only contact.
Your letters were read and your incoming mail was opened.
It was hard. It is hard.
My father?
Imprisoned by the British Government
for taking up arms against the British.
1921.
Dublin.
Those who serve some kind of a prison sentence don't talk a lot.
They don't talk.
On my mother's side, my uncle was shot...
The simple life has gone.

On Bold Street Eric said:
The first five rows in Anfield were benches.
You went to the kiosk—and you'd offer coins or jam jars
and you'd get a big metal tally with a hole
in the middle and when you went down the steps
the usherette had a big leather belt
and she threaded these tallies to her belt...
By the time the film was starting
this girl would be weighed down with metal tallies.
They were quite heavy, you know.

A corn-porter and his wife in a house on
Heaton Street said to a reporter
of the Liverpool Journal in November 1849:
How do we live on six shillings, and five of us?
We just strive to live.
We have not a shilling in the house.
We have trust at a small shop;
but if we cannot meet the bill on a Saturday night
then we have no more credit.

6

1871: PARIS COMMUNE

St Patrick's day. I see the police before I see the march. The
band looks like it is playing out through the doors of the old Irish
Center at the Wellington Rooms. Closed now. I danced there
in the 1980s with doctors from Africa, Ireland, students from
Communist Hungary. The black berets and banners lit by an early
afternoon unexpected sunlight on Hope Street. Larkin Liverpool.
Che Guevara Liverpool. Signs and signals of solidarity and of
despair. As I pass the Everyman Theatre, a balcony closed to the
public is filled with staff who watch the Irish in Liverpool perform
being Irish in Liverpool. They pass the stone sculpture luggage of
emigrants where an Irish leprechaun lifts himself onto a suitcase
to film the parade. Tricolors and Irish flags fade into St James'
Cemetery. Do the Famine Refugees hear the music still? Do they
feel the colors of their once imagined Republic burning through
this sunlight?

Walking between the cemetery and the prison, I go in search
of Robert Tressell whose birth home above Paddy Power on
Camden Street Dublin I passed every day all my life ago thinking
about Liverpool; a paupers grave, the unnamed, unmarked
revolutionary dead.

The smell of hot cross buns over Walton Jail. A car hoots a certain
pattern of sound. Coded communications to the cells where women

smashed their prison windows. They signal back, waving into history. Do we see the activists disguised as orange sellers as we pass the Conservative Club on Dale Street? It's broken glass smoothed into the flyover. Do we remember their suffrage protest now? At Toxteth Library on the evening of the Referendum to leave the European Union, the woman in front of me says: "I don't know which way to vote." "I don't even know what we are voting for," her friend answers.

Headlines and News for April 1847:
"Liverpool's story is the world's glory."

"At St Mary's Cambridge St and St Martins in the Field, Vauxhall. 7,350 buried Irish paupers."

"Crowds gather each day in Mount Pleasant to watch the bodies of the dead fever victims being removed to the pauper cemetery near the workhouse in Cambridge Street."

"New fever sheds to be built in buildings in Great Howard St in Vauxhall on the corner with Chadwyck Street."

"Passengers riding in coaches from Bootle to Liverpool insisted that the vehicles bypass the fever sheds." *Liverpool Mercury,* 8 June 1847.

"The *Akbar* and *Newcastle* and *Druid* will be used as Fever vessels— a quarantine station for infected Irish arriving on steamers from Irish ports. Twice a day, a steamer attended at the Albert Dock conveyed fever victims into the river and onto one of the ships."

"On Lace Street it is reported one third of inhabitants have died— 472 people—so far."

On Brownlow Hill Grace said:
From 1978 to 1984 I was a nurse on the docks
They had churches on ships then.

On Hardwick Street Seamus said:
The Night of Broken Glass, children were sent to safety
by their parents
and their parents were never seen again.
They arrived in a place by Dover
the board of guardians
took children to be looked after
by guardians in Liverpool.

On Water Street the Lord Mayor said:
He arrived through Clarence Dock
and was admitted into the workhouse.
If the doors had not been open here to my great grandfather
as a Famine Refugee
then he would not have survived;
my family would have died out then.
It wasn't rich people helped him survive.
It was the poor.

An emaciated workman at the Exchange Flags
said to a reporter in November 1849:
"I'm ashamed at going home time after time with nothing."

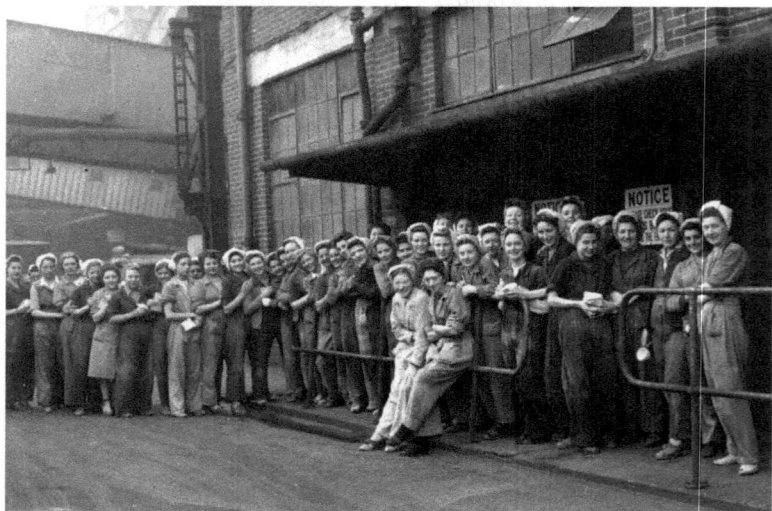

7

1911: LIVERPOOL GENERAL STRIKE

Borders are a state of mind.

The day after the Referendum. All day I cannot settle. I walk.
Pointless small tasks. Watching the fallout. I see Rosa Luxemburg's
manifesto. Beckett's *Watt*. I hear Simone de Beauvoir saying on
Bold Street: "The war is over but its corpse stretches all over the
world. There is not a grave big enough to bury it."

My mother's sister uncovered all the children's drawings, jokes,
poems; the writing beneath the wallpaper. I cut slices out of that
wall. Build a monument. Proof that Angela Feeney lived there.
Aged 12, I had called for her. Stood outside that Catholic front
door waiting before we got the number ten bus to the Bluecoat.
Unrestrained socialism in black lace gloves; our questions for
writers; artists of our own lives.

1979: I am holding the telephone for my grandmother while my
mother goes into the kitchen; or did I just walk down the stairs and
pick up the phone in the hallway? I sit on the stairs in between the
ancestors who were waiting to hear my mother's conversation.
I fall far into a darkness that has all the texture of place. Two elderly
women were talking. "We must be interesting!" one said laughing as
they realized someone else was on the line.

Steve told me that when he was at a boarding school for the blind in the 1950s: "I used to hang the radio out through one of the toilet windows to pick up the Everton match." At night as abandoned darkness closed in: "I would tune the radio into the police—listen to their emergencies throughout the night." Spaces are like rock-fall that we collapse down into; a quickening moment of chance.

I saw an old photograph of my mother once. I just came across it in a Liverpool local history book—she was walking across an opening between blocks of flats holding hands with her first born three children. A woman in the prime of her life. "The free woman is just being born." A *tableau* of her own self she would never see.

Walking down Eldon Street looking out to St Joseph's I photograph the last bell the Italians heard before they were deported. The dispossessed cross over rubbish at Great Homer Street, carrying plastic bags from the remnant memory of a market that their ancestors once spoke of. There are traces of refugees everywhere in this city: Famine roads, a cobbled lane so clearly delineated it leads to less than nowhere now. Eldon Street, Lime Kiln Lane, Horatio Street—the view of the dome the sailors must have seen—more distant than the world.

> It harrows me with fear and wonder.
> What art thou that usurp'st this time of night
> Stay! Speak, speak! I charge thee speak!

I stand on the exact spot near the altar their twenty-year old selves stood. Wexford, Clonmel, Carlow still coursing through their voices and letters home. "I would conversate with Johnny Morris." August 1914. A time to marry and to say goodbye. Two women sit at the back of St Anthony's of Egypt on Scotland Road. They unwrap sweets and hold on to their trolleys and prayer books, touching holy pictures; they pray and pray again. A man walks to the front alter—bows, lights a candle then moves from one shrine of candles to the next and repeats his benediction. St Anthony, St Joseph; my grandmother Lily Leary must have prayed to these same effigies. What did she pray for? Did the lord hear her prayers? Blundell. A glass stained with slavery. Sands of Egypt.

Their intimate lives reveal themselves to me now only in the nights when census records were taken in the long ago: my great grandfather out on the ships; his son visiting his grandmother; a woman abandoned looking after the children of the house. Their secrets almost invisible now.

So many ghosts came across from the cemetery last night. I must have left the attic window open. There was a time when we lived on Moscow Drive, I would journey the city with them looking into the foundations of darkness; a beam of wood with rope marks; the last vestige of slave ships moored at the old dry dock.

On Lime Street Brian said:
I've seen it now on his birth certificate.
"Plasterer's assistant."
He and his brother moved to Liverpool from Luca in Tuscany.
They were set to work on the lions outside St George's Hall.

On County Road the Butcher said:
In twenty odd years when I came round here
every shop was open.
You look around here now and
every shop is nearly all shutted up . . .
You can't produce extra money.

On Liberty Street Zac said:
I was born in Liverpool,
have been here all my life.

On Leopold Street Hadinet said:
I started reading avidly.
George Orwell, Jack London,
biographies of the great Labour leaders,
the life story of Trotsky.
I just read and read and read.

On the Goree Piazza Kathy said:
He was 14. He was in Canada on a farm.
I got his papers and it was like he had no parents . . .
She was a single mum
sending letters asking about his whereabouts
he's passing letters to the same organization
and they are not passing them.
He actually put a notice in the newspaper
an appeal in the Liverpool Echo
but me nan had died by then
so she never got to see her brother.
Who are people to make those decisions?

8

1916: EASTER RISING

There is always a moment when something is said and I am already under ice. I sense the spaces between each word . . . a question that closes doors. That Francoesque conservative Catholicism. I glimpse its edges again in the far distances of Calvary on a hillside in Salamanca.

I have no voice here. Family is always the first and most sacred sanctuary. "Your mum and dad." "Your daughter." Family: the where, the when . . . The judgement in other people's eyes.

1997 Sister Mary Vincent: "When are you going to stop all this?"

1986 Sister Mary Carmel: "This is Home Economics: how to cook for your family and for your husband."

Your profession?
Orpheus: Poet
What do you mean by "poet"?
Orpheus: To write, without being a writer.

Rain. A whistle. Drums. Something is emerging off stage. The city stops. The Orange Lodge begin to march again.

When did Moses Leary stop following the news from *home*? When did Michael Quinn stop knowing the price of oats in Dromore?

Each night I dream another version of family. A world making and unmaking itself. A bed I must lie in.

Concrete and empty. The doorway makes no sense as she crosses from one hounded dereliction into another.

Liverpool. It began as seven streets shaped as a H. H Block 1981. Expulsion from a Spanish class will follow when she shows solidarity in a letter to a Catalan pen pal. Sister Mary Carmen said: "My father was in prison during the Civil War." A guidebook remembers: "In 1207, King John founded the port of Liverpool to supply soldiers to Ireland, newly conquered."

Even when someone does not die from attempting suicide, a kind of death takes place. She breathed in grief as though she had buried him, photographing the city like a crime scene. Wexford. But where in Wexford? So many Learys. How does that line lead all the way to ... "We were out at Mass." That word "Mass" seemed important in the half-told story of that night. Hearing Spanish spoken for the first time in Seville, she read *Ulysses* as though it was all the voice she had.

Eighteenth century views—ships, fields, ropes. In December 1989, did the city look just as it looked last night? Three men at intervals of fifteen minutes stumble an uncertain line as though their bodies weigh more than they do. Was that crossroads in front of Duke Street the same all those years ago? Did the lights at the crossings still change? She sees a small figure moving herself from a wheelchair into a bed. Lights off. Lights on: a waiting room of women smoking. Watching TV. Talking. A friend of her mother's was on duty that night her waters broke. Another humiliation; it felt like no comfort. I turn away, unable to watch this last breaking of her spirit.

"I like to go to church at 12:30." She must be there now. The
routines old women keep with themselves. Where will our journey
in conversation lead us? Cecily takes me back through the war to
a brother rescued from tornado bombing. To an uncle driven mad
by violence of war in Italy. A lover who became her husband; she
touches her arm, fixing a part of her sleeve that does not need
adjusting. "I'm a long time without him." "Move out the way of that
doorway and come down here. If a bomb drops you'll block the way
and we won't be able to get out." She laughs as she recalls her sister's
voice cajoling their own father to stop looking out of the shelter at
the sky and to come in with them. There was something about that
proximity to place that startled me. Everywhere she walked in this
conversation was where we sat. She had seen her whole life in this
house; from that chair. Ninety-seven years. Standing across from
my nana in Hades: all the answers I forgot to hear.

Q: December 8th. "The Immaculate Conception"? Not "immaculate"
but devoid somehow. The day preoccupies me. I am standing in
Blacklers on the corner of Elliot Street and Great Charlotte Street
in front of a china horse and cart that we buy for our mother. I pass
the ghost of my grandmother.

A: That child your mother is holding up to the window
You are standing on the outside of your own life
You saw this at two years old

I was there just a short while and yet have been in that room on
Leinster Road saying nothing at all, just breathing in their lives all
of my life.

That moment with my grandmother returned with each winter. It
is a dark November night and a secret conversation is held in the
back of the car while the leaves gather in rain on the windscreen; my
mother has just stepped out "on a message" to collect a mass card.

"Don't let them take your child away from you," her mother said to me. The difference between listening and hearing.

We all grow up in small enclaves, she thought.

On Old Hall Street Melville said:
Taking out my map,
I found that Old Hall Street was marked there,
through its whole extent with my father's pen;
a thousand fond, affectionate emotions rushed around my heart.
Yes, in this very street, thought I, nay,
on this very flagging my father walked.
Then I almost wept . . .
little did he think, that a son of his would ever visit Liverpool
as a poor friendless sailor boy.
But I was not born then: no, when he walked this flagging,
I was not so much as thought of;
I was not included in the census of the universe.
My own father did not know me then.

9

1917: RUSSIAN REVOLUTION

Our parents and ancestors absorb the changes in this city, living inside routines that they own. The pattern of their lives belonged to them like the maps of disappeared streets. Music played in one house was danced to in living rooms across the road. "These patterns used to baffle and exclude me," she thought. The huddle of cloaks on Galway Bay. Women in Connemara shawled against the otherness of those that are not them.

In a dark room I see the night-time of a stranger's return. The phone call that he made on discovering two children lying there alone. That house at the top right-hand corner of a road shaped like a keyhole. A tree like night. The first black leaves I had ever seen.

They moved house quickly when she was away. Counted the rooms. Took the child and closed the door making sure that the keys of the mother did not fit. The locket she left was hidden or lost. The matching bit of cloth burnt on the fire as soon as they were sure she'd gone.

A fine mist over the River Mersey. Late morning. Almost noon. In front of Chinatown the Lodge did a full band rendition of God Save the Queen. She closed the window and went back to bed with the *Liverpool Chronicle* of 1822; huge skirmishes in Dublin with the Orange Lodge tying an orange lily to the top of the Bank of Ireland. How quickly the Irish Parliament had been relegated in

name. Was the lily placed there as a sign of victory? The Union
further defined with the disbanding of the Irish parliament? A
child pretends to skate on the spot on the corner of Back Roscoe
Street (where her ancestor from Clonmel had been a shoemaker).
Half-term. The city seems half asleep. Origins and patterns of
becoming.

A triangle.

"I knew there was a triangle it was dangerous for me to cross,"
Michelle said.

Ray said: "I was walking along the street and on the other side was
a young black woman. The police van trailed slower than her pace.
All the way down the road. That van followed her."

I thought about the walls in Belfast. Peace walls. Exclusion zones.
Places she knew not to go to. In the '70s. In the '80s.

A Family History Group volunteer in the library explained: "She
discovered that her sister was her mother and her mother was her
grandmother. She went with her adoptive mother to meet her real
mother. The adoptive mother stayed outside and after half an hour
she went in and said: 'I just wanted to say thank you for giving me
my daughter.'"

Joyce said: "It is for the still-borns that the mothers come to look.
They just want to find a grave where they can go and lay flowers.
They were never told where they were buried. Two sisters came
in yesterday, they must have been in their sixties and one of them
wanted to find where her child had been buried."

St Luke's. A day darkening on our decisions.
My father stares through
bombed-out
windows.

Someone is missing.
He is waiting, watching. A granddaughter is married. The mother
arrives years later into the ruins. The blue sky reflecting into her
Spanish red on black. Amber light hits the Liver Building; two
clock-faces beat out the time that was in it.

"This was me when I arrived in Liverpool." A young man from
Eretria smiles out of a snowy landscape. "This was the first time
I had seen snow." Philip in remembering said: "It's the hope that
kills you." He takes me to the docks. It is 1901 and his own great
grandfather has just arrived in from Guyana. Saved the life of a boy
drowning in the Liverpool canal. Had a street named after him. In
the Lord Mayor's office at the Liver Building later that day, I see a
paperweight James Larkin, arms outstretched to the River Mersey.

On Jermyn Street Michelle said:
The Toxteth triangle.
Outside of those boundaries
the race riots.
you couldn't pass that boundary
into Kenny
by the ice rink.
On Prescot Road
another boundary of the triangle.
You stayed
within
your zone.
An Irish community,
An Italian community.
In the 70s, it felt like that for me.
You'd stay even within the periphery.
If you hear the stories
of the families
who lived in those areas,
it's kind of torrid.

On Great Crosshall Street Ray said: Every time I go up Bold Street.
In that war memorial by the Lyceum.
Look for the black face and you won't find one . . .

10

1936: SPANISH CIVIL WAR

In later years, I would secretly encounter my mother walking with one of the patients from the closed asylum through the avenues of that park. "Care in the community." What was Liverpool then? . . . A convent door that I would knock on. A Sister of Mercy with a heavy fountain pen that looked like it was made of precious metals. I watched her write out the numbers I was to decode without knowing why. You could see it in the way the grasses sloped gently down. A hidden glass conservatory. The others would drive their children along their private road into and out of electric gates. The pristine colors of their day glimpsed through railings. The sunshine in their hair. Something different about these children. Prep school. Grammar school. The same nuns who taught us changed shape when they sighted grammar-school girls in the wooded avenues of their memory that traveled all the way to Salamanca. Had she backed Franco to the hilt? Had his death caused a prayer in mourning? Inside that paneled room of the convent I walk the length of their silence.

As he spoke about what he remembered she watched Indian Partition: a wishing well of women falling.

On the way back to the ferry, I chat with a man whose father was a captain. I talk with another man minutes later who had sailed the route between Russia and Poland. They stare out at the River Mersey and across to Liverpool. One is waiting for a boat he knows is due to set sail; the other waits for a fish. "I caught a dogfish with my son last Sunday. I got divorced last year." The other man whose father was a captain, watches out still for his father's ship: "He was on the SS Atlantic Conveyer that went down in the Falklands."

Liverpool ships navigated a trade predicated on slavery.
An iPhone factory in China installs safety nets to catch suicides before they land.

The freedom trains in 1989 had already started to bring over thousands. What can I remember about that time? Moscow Drive. The Moscow campaign. Moscow withdrawing its support from the East. Lost now inside the fog. "I could have been living in a village in Ireland in the 1830s, the place I was in. Liverpool in 1989 was not unlike that village," I hear myself speak to a future listener, the aftermath of reports published.

Where exactly had they imagined they might hide her? "Magdalene asylums . . . became homes for unmarried mothers and 'wayward' daughters . . . removing these 'shameful objects' from public view."

Maori shapes; green gemstones. I would glimpse them like Christmas. Their powers of hiding dispossession sat next to the whiskey my father poured late into the night in the hours before he would wake to whatever building site or dockyard he hoped would choose him. In the 1950s, while working his passage across the seas as a chippy, he purchased a small plot in New Zealand. Did that land stay inside his body like another life lived under a different climate? Sometimes important letters would be placed at the side of a glass in the cabinet that I stood cleaning the night before it was sold and I was admitted into Mill Road maternity hospital: handwritten news that had traveled a distance from Ireland, Ethiopia, Ghana.

The old workhouse opposite Brome Terrace was Mill Road; a
workhouse made into a maternity hospital. A Belfast woman
remembered: "The workhouse was sometimes known as the
poorhouse. It was for the homeless and for women who fell by the
wayside... Women who were pregnant had to work until the babies
were born. Usually, people who went to the workhouse never left it
until they died. Children of inmates were made to work very hard
in the laundries."

In my mind it all happened in an afternoon—there was some
change of plan. I was wheeled out into a corridor where I thought
I saw
my mother.

She woke in
a corridor.
a cut so deep she could not breathe.
Was I asked something? Did I speak?

Across a phone line to Ireland I try to remember what my name is.
A ghost of a woman watches the new woman, the free woman that
is just being born.

An intimate landscape where daily routine is transmitted at the
distance of generations. "She usually goes to mass at that time..."
My daughter translates my mother's timetable, her daily routine
overheard from Ireland.

The Irish Times, November 1989: "East Berlin ... an elderly man strode
back and forth on numerous occasions across a white line which
separated East from West. On the bridge, a woman raced forward
good-humouredly towards the crossing, as if trying to escape."

Falling down into a townland, a parish, a plot of nine acres. Three widows letting, subletting, never owning. Lives as lost as their unmarried names. The records of the Omagh District Asylum noted: "Mary Quinn escaped from laundry on the evening of 15 December but was not missed till bedtime... she escaped again on the 24th, but was brought back in an hour... The laundress came before the Board and stated she nor her assistants were aware of the escape of Mary Quinn... The door of the laundry was kept locked except when women were obliged to go out for the purpose of carrying in bedding."

My maternal ancestor Mary Quinn of Dromore in a letter to her son Michael in Liverpool February 1887 wrote: "I am not long for this world. You would not know me I am so failed. Soon I will be mingling with the angels in heaven . . . I walk through this empty house . . . "

Mother: "Your nan was brought up by her grandmother."
Daughter: "Yes, but her mother was dead. I am not dead."

In this city Congolese dogs have two faces;
Liver Birds glance back into the future from which they cannot fly.

But what if the lock was never unlocked? What if the key fell as she walked away? Would she recognize my face still? Would she know her own? Keys that lock and unlock. A torn peacock fabric; the picture will be complete when he comes home from sea and finds me. "Do you think he can see us in all this darkness?" asked the daughter as the Irish actor performed a French play on the London stage.

"You must have cake in" said Mr Lin to my nana in Victoria Gardens. "Someone will call today and the first thing he will say is . . ." It was 1946 when Mary Quinn's great grandson returned from France. But this is not 1946 and this is not 1919 and we cannot

blame the war for all this damage of life; wounds of time cried out
through the fog of the indented quarry that is Lime Street.

I gaze at plot 10 that is not a cemetery; it is a mark on a map
where three widows leased and sublet their lives. A walk away
from the Female National School. Three fields from the Corn
Mill. Suddenly that empty house in Ireland where a woman writes
in mourning for the lost life of her daughter-in-law, her widowed
son, his derelict children in Liverpool—suddenly that house
seems crowded with disappearances and short-term rent. To her
son in Liverpool Mary Quinn wrote: "Frank is hired out . . . The
melancholy is upon him. Don't mention it if you write back."

After the Berlin Wall came down
A daughter said:
"Where is my mother? It was my brother who told them about her."

In a maternity ward in Liverpool in 1989 Miranda said: "Alack,
what trouble / was I then to you?" and Prospero answered: "Oh, a
cherubim / Thou wast that did preserve me."

"Those moments in which a token of the future lies hidden." The
statues in the *Jardin du Luxembourg*. The Polish Resistance producing
a newspaper in Paris that would be found half a century later and
'harvested' back into the destroyed library of its people. A translation
in time. At Portbou he could not find his way back to the border . . .

I retrace Walter Benjamin's steps across the rubble of a long-ago
exile. "To transmute a glance" from this side of the Wall to the other,
to those whose lives will be made in another elsewhere. In the Berlin
Zoo I watch him watching the otter in the rain. I follow his footsteps
as he arrives in memory at a monument to something that is not love.
I wait in the years after the records are destroyed and watch as they
are remade under the urgent questions of the newly made citizen.
On this site, here in the derelict remade grounds of the workhouse

where Mary Quinn did not escape with the laundry I find my earliest memory:

Holding the baby, I climb across the rubble of the hospital car park. I say hello to the surgeon as she passes. She does not recognize me. I was yesterday's emergency. No emergency now.

On Exmouth Place John said:
Liverpool is
a rollercoaster ride from going right up there as
second metropolis;
second city of empire
and
then
that
incredible
collapse
down
to
shocked city
post
industrial
post
colonial
Britain.

On Myrtle Street Brenda said:
African sailors
used to get off the ships and
they would walk in a line
one behind the other
through the village of Seaforth
just looking at the shops
buying an ice-cream
and then they would go back to the ship.

11

1942: THE RESISTANCE

In a far-away wood she gave birth. Removing a brick from the wall, she rested the baby who breathed in his last of 1831. In the next field people harvesting loaned her a child and a spade to dig. "It is alive," cried the child hearing the child cry. After court she waited the night out, wondering to what part of the far world away from this field, from that spade, from the filled gap in a church wall she would be transported. And what about that paradisaical otherworld that the pre-medieval Irish sailed through?

In the *Tiergarten,* Walter Benjamin said: He who seeks to approach his own buried past must conduct himself like a man digging.

The question often asked and never fully understood is: something about time passing, children growing; a pointlessness raining down and clearing the air. Stumbling into the street with a suitcase and no means of securing a place to live, a job. Always any job. Always a suitcase.

Standing on vigil through the years in the Walker Art Gallery. Waiting for a train. Another departure. Not sure why she is leaving; just knowing she is not welcome to stay. All the schools she visited in all the cities. All the houses with all the rooms.

In 1943 Jean Guéhenno wrote in his diary: "Renan said there was no use demanding freedom all the time. Just begin, he said, by thinking freely."

Who were the Suffragettes convicted in that winter of 1909? Orange sellers in disguise. I began the day looking for the faces of the Mujeres Libres who left Liverpool to fight in the Spanish Civil War. Instead, I find photographs of the women arrested during the Paris Commune.

"If you had been born in a different time, that might have happened to you." To be burnt at the stake. I think of the aunt just home from the missions exploring with her religious counterparts where to hide the child that was me and the child that was about to be born. "That was a peculiar idea," Paul reflected decades later: "most girls and women were sent from Ireland not to Ireland." Did Dickens think about the cells beneath his feet as he spoke at St George's Hall? A trapdoor beneath his words falling from the page down into the cells from fiction to autobiography.

Back to the docks:
the death house, cages where suicides can be seen and claimed; seen and forgotten . . .
All the voices.

I hear the storm outside. Mick has another shift on the tugboat before Sunday will begin. Sunday. "You would have been burned at the stake as a witch," says the doctor in September 1989 to the working-class pregnant girl, her legs wide open and raised in stirrups on a table. He points to a mark just beneath her left breast that she had never seen before and that she cannot possibly see from that position. Standing at the crossroads. Outside of the village. I leave the hospital before the rain starts again.

At Liverpool docks they disappear forever. I retrace their footsteps to Strokestown and out to the disappeared townland that was their land. After the final eviction notice in 1848, James Connor of Ballykilcline said to the magistrate: "Their will be done and not mine."

Recording the Citizen section from *Ulysses* with the sacked dockers in the Casa on Hope Street: "We will have Europe again." Afterwards, Mick reads his timetable schedule for this week—out on the river. "There are no boats now," she says. "There are," he replies, "it's just that people don't see them." Early hours of the morning. A clock with six faces. The only one in the world. "We are the only city that does not own its river. Peel Holdings. As a Union we cannot negotiate with them. Nothing to negotiate," Tony concludes.

Am I saying a reluctant farewell; taking a last glance across Hades before I leave again? Are the connections between Ireland and Liverpool real? I see two lights of China Town and remember this time last week when the Orange Lodge stopped and played God Save the Queen. Can they hear these Anglican bells on the other side of the road at the Catholic Cathedral? Is anyone really listening? What night flight am I getting tonight? Where am I going? What is the point of looking out at a river where no boats pass? I am only half here. The city is only half here.

A man pushes a pram down Upper Duke Street, the wheels have little flashing lights. He has gloves on and a coat and he walks with a group: mother, father, child; mother, father, another child. They look like they have somewhere to go. They look like they are in the middle of the October Sunday of their lives. I can almost feel the pattern of their evening. Something of the inner lights of their homes show through their winter coats as they stroll down the hill into "town."

Lorca's La Barraca
Taking theater to remote villages
Calderon's *Life is a Dream.*
A story you half glanced. A station of the cross . . . What life was
passed here? The train goes backwards.

Why am I going over it all now? I think about Eric aged 91 as he
revisits 1934 searching for the disappeared marks of the goalpost
he painted on his street wall in Anfield.

Yesterday I felt banished and exiled from all this. Today I stand in
the kitchen and watch my father make tea. Tea leaves and fortunes
of sugar.

File notes on children to be deported from a care home in
Liverpool to work on farms in French-speaking Canada:

Father: "a demobilized soldier."
Father: "supposed to be in County Down Ireland."
Father: "dead."
Mother: "alive."
Reason: "a drunken parent."

And what of those who disappear?

Visitor: "He ran away from Mr X and has not been found since."
Farmer: "Send us another."

Questions on form to be ticked by care home:
Does it have good teeth?
Is it moral?
Is it baptized?

Sometimes we hear a little of the children's thoughts in words
scrawled in letters "home":
"I think I have a good chance of having a place of my own some day
and showing the world what Liverpudlians can do."

9 August 1907: "I think I would go to England when I am big to pass the boat. When I pass the boat I was very much afraid."

"I wonder just what Liverpool looks like today."

Joseph remembered the journey out from Liverpool: "During 1922 there were two more parties of kids sent to Canada—We were each given a comb and the Holy Bible. We sailed in the S.S. Regina on the 31st May ... The passengers were from all parts of Europe—there were Polish people, Germans, Ukrainians, Russians, Bulgarians, Czechoslovakians, Scandinavians, and British. It was amazing to hear all the different languages. They were all poor, the unwanted of Europe, going to try their luck in a new land ... The crew of the ship seemed to go out of their way to make the voyage enjoyable, especially for the kids from Liverpool. For most of the crew it was their home port ... They organized games for the kids and I remember how good they were with the kids of the Europeans whose language they didn't know."

Letter from a child to priest who helped to deport her:

"Dear Father, I write you this letter to let you know that I have found my sister. I was very glad when I got a letter from her ... I have finished the *Catholic Fireside* and would like to have more if you have some. I am very well were [*sic*] I stay. I talk the French very much ... I learn about Our Father, The Hail Mary and the Apostles Creed and the Confession of Sinners. I would like to no [*sic*] of father and mother if you could send me the news of them if you please father I would like to no if they are dead or alive I would like to send them news of me and my sister."

File notes on a child who had been deported from a care home in Liverpool and who was working on a farm in French-speaking Canada: "He is a good boy."

In the first year his health is good and the religious visitor ticks
each box of the report "yes" and "no" in all the right places.
The next year the report reads:
"He seemed to be losing his mind."
"He cannot tell me his name."
"When he does speak, it is impossible to understand him."
"He does not even answer to his own name."

"Have the boat met in Liverpool. Have the boy handed to you
then arrange for the boy's disposal."

Dream after leaving Cruit Island in Donegal and arriving back into
Dublin: I am being made to disappear... we half communicated,
half heard, half understood.

What does it mean to have been born a woman? "I am born on 12
July 1972." There is no story here. What did Tony say to me at the
Alliance Française on Kildare Street? Begin there, begin when you
went to the library. There seem to be two beginnings to this story.
All my words find their etymology in exile.

On Whitechapel Mary said:
The morning I left to enter the convent my father
had left me a letter on the kitchen table:
"I hope everything goes well for you and you'll be happy."

On Aigburth Drive Yozzer Hughes in Boys from the Blackstuff *said:*
I thought I knew where I was goin'. I know I'm to blame.
But what I wanna know is: is this all there is?
Down to this?
For the rest of my life?
Everything I've ever wanted and all the things I thought I had.
They've all been taken away.

On Triumph Way Francesca said:
The baby died.
And the court said: what was the baby's name?
"Thomas."
On board for Tasmania
Her conduct on the boat was reported as "good."

FEMALE ROAD SWEEPERS MAR 2 191

12

1945: V–DAY

He was taken off Uaigh Island. Had survived that long without electricity. *Uaigh*: cave. Before the Famine there were how many people living there? After 1971 there were none. The schoolhouse abandoned. He spoke nothing but a few broken sentences all his life. If he had stayed there, how would the horses have made their way across the battlefields in 1916? How would the Learys' from Enniscorthy have heard each other talking down the phone lines from Anfield sharing stories about their ever-afters?

I visit him when everyone is gone . . . drink a dark corner cup of hospital tea with my mother. I can't remember what he said. If we said anything. Gabriel texted me from New York: "Just being there with him is enough. Speaking is not important."

Back down the road in the city library, I listen to what other people say they are searching for as I fast forward through lives on microfilm: "There was no grave. They didn't mark where he was buried. He was my brother. Died four hours old just after I was born in 1953." What am I looking for? . . . just speaking names out loud to a family research volunteer (who has my father's eyes) feels like a betrayal of something. What is it that I do not know? What is it that I search out in all these destroyed court housing plans? Whose face am I looking to find in photographs? Moments of recognition. I see the village in these photographs and film reels.

Postcards home. What stories do I need? When. When seems to be important. When and where. Where did they come from before they were here? When did they leave? The roads stop in County Tyrone, Sligo, Clonmel, Wexford. My ancestors trail Famine Roads through Land Wars; finding their way into Liverpool. Two of my ancestors arrive on the same boat into Liverpool out of different Irelands. How did they survive? How do I survive? There is no story here.

This city belongs to them. To those who live in the villages they were born into. This city belongs to them. At the corner of *Boulevard Saint-Germain* and *Rue Saint-Benoît,* Jean Paul Sartre said: "Families naturally prefer widows to unmarried mothers, but only just."

The African and Irish doctors speak their otherness at the shared space of our family tea table. Ghana, the Congo, Sierra Leone, Liverpool. Later Ethiopian Famine would transform our front living room into a refugee aid centre. Blankets knitted by the old women who would later knit for the baby. After the *ceilidh* in the Wellington Rooms, I dance past the framed effigy of James Connolly in the doorway.

On the feast of the Immaculate Conception in 1965, thirty-three years after my mother was born, the clerical regalia was placed under glass at a distance of fire regulated adoration. Did she suddenly begin to hear the language of what she was praying? I remember a cave inside a doorway. "You spoke Latin before you spoke English." I watched the ancestors glance the corner shadows of their longing as I walked with her into incense.

At the *Café de Flore,* Simone de Beauvoir said: I realized that the first question to come up was *What has it meant to me to be a woman?*

In the offices of Liverpool One Miles said:
My impression when we were doing our first leasing here was:
"This is a grand city but how come the economics just doesn't stack up?"

On Lower Breck Road David said:
I always intended to go home. I was proper homesick.
I wanted to go home but going home I was thrown back to square one.

On Boundary Lane Doreen said:
Your husband would come in, he'd bring home the bacon and
you'd cook it. We weren't the little woman. It's how it was.
Then during the Lock-Out with them men, there was a pride
and a respect for what the women were doing.
A woman could be away on a delegation
or out on the picket line
and they'd say: "So and so said to me today 'how do you make gravy?'
'If you put a pie in, what number do you put the oven on?'"

13

1956: HUNGARIAN UPRISING

My story is broken twice by ghosts.

My father said: "I remember seeing my grandmother walking through the hall in Langham Street with a black shawl around her shoulders."

Waking in another language; hidden under cloaks. Tracy in the front path sits in her wheelchair watching our long summers disappear. Aged four, I would bend my body in to hear her affectionate sounds; broken dry lips breathing in long pauses. Waiting. Waiting. The widows talk with a five-year-old Catherine; rooms emptied of everything but dark wood stolen from Africa. After school I would be sent across the road or next door; running messages, keeping the old women company. Entering into the silence of their departing lives. Crossing two centuries we sat together through each late afternoon—the time of day that stretches into but is not yet evening and that the Spanish have a name for.

WALKING

On Erskine Street Brendan said:
I started in the docks when I was sixteen.
My dad was a dock worker when
the Union derecognized shop stewards.

On Great Newton Street Ivanna said:
You don't forget where you come from.

On Waterloo Road Mike said:
I don't remember anyone in the official Union saying
how magnificent it was that we blockaded uranium hexafluoride
from entering or leaving Liverpool dock.

On Cherry Lane Peter said:
It was in 1916
my father and my uncle
were persecuted.
Our German surname changed.

On Adlam Road Maya said:
I was born in Bombay India, and he goes:
You look like my people. I'm from Iran.
I said: My grandfather's family tree traces us back
to that Caspian Sea area.

14

1968: CIVIL RIGHTS MARCH, DERRY & FRENCH
SOCIAL REVOLUTION

Ghosts. We did not visit our dead. No rituals of grave decoration. The dead went on living with us. Their lives, their sayings, the names passed down through generations whose love for one another is so intense it makes breathing almost impossible. The Irish woman who lived in the house was my mother's grandmother. "Me Nin" told a fairy-tale closer to Tyrone than Liverpool; shrouded in a blanket her refrain rested in the same opening and closing of stories that De Valera failed to collect in 1937. Those who had left were gone to the Free State; those from the now North were disappeared forever.

The grandmother grieved to the child in the late November when the Wall had fallen. They huddled close together in a darkness at the back of the yellow car; the woman who was mother, daughter and grandmother-to-be had just stepped out into winter to buy a mass card: "Don't let them take your child away from you."

Together we passed into Hades. It was some time after three and before five. My mother stepped into church "to collect a mass card," and while she was out of the car, yellow leaves and red leaves gathered on the windscreen. I sat with my grandmother who wiped her eyes as we visited her first-born son who had died in 1932 of pneumonia. "The council came and took the roof off the flat where we were staying—in the middle of winter." Did she say something about Sligo? "Where had the Walshes come from?"

On Wood Street Joan said:
I think it's done a huge amount.
You can't underestimate how important that's been.
The people who conducted themselves with such dignity
for a generation—that's an extraordinary achievement.
I think people outside Liverpool joke about Liverpool's clannishness.
They've stopped joking about it now.

On Kirkby Bank Road Irina said:
"Managed decline" we were the ones that got the vicious end of that way
of thinking: "those people don't matter, they're not important,
they don't vote Tory and so we're not interested."

On Pilgrim Street Dylan said:
Oh that was a wonderful little shop. Just a house now.

On Leinster Road Joe said:
It had become a glimmering girl.

On Regent Road Rhiannon said:
We won't be here much longer. China is taking over the market
in metal recycling.

On Canal Street Zada said:
I wonder where that boat's going?

On Shore Road a sailor just off a ship said:
We need a cash machine to change money.

15

1989: THE FALL OF THE BERLIN WALL

The Berlin Wall was not yet dismantled. Inside and outside of the
confession box "the priest and God see everything." Counting and
avoiding the cracks in-between the paving stones, I take my time and
step carefully along Town Row. I pass up and along Donegal Road,
Ulster Road, Belfast Road, Leinster Road. My mother said: "I think
me mam's nin was from Sligo." They never went back. Not even in
their minds. They never returned. Children without shoes begging
on the buses and trams in the years when the Free State became the
first Republic. That was all her mother would remember when forced
to remember something out loud about Ireland. They never went
back. Sometimes she thought that they would never have even left
the front step of their village homes other than to go to church or to
the brother's house around the corner or to visit the daughter next
door with food. Journeys out felt like expeditions into the world of
the known but still distant city. To buy a mass card, to take a message,
to collect children, to post a letter—

But where was that letter being posted to?

She remembered: opening a letter that she had been asked to post
that her mother had written to her second born daughter. Thin blue
tracing paper that marked a time when words carried weight that
translated into the cost of its journey out into the world. She knew
that she would see her own name mentioned: something about how X
"is settling a little". She knew she was a stranger in this land. X.

A woman who cannot write her own name. X her female ancestor
Sarah Quinn: I glance the black mark of her hand on microfilm.

To pass through Castlederg that night was to remember the Orange
Lodge marching through the lives of so many. "Me dad used to
hide us in the upstairs room and lock all the windows and doors."
"They would stand outside the front door and bang their drums. It
was terrifying." To pass the police barricade in Castlederg was to
remember that it was impossible to pass that barricade or to travel
that road before. To pass by Paisley's Church was to remember his
voice beating our years into darkness across a televised version of
what became history.

Famine Refugees. We carry the memory of their arrival into
Clarence Dock and bury our thoughts in the foundations of the Old
Dock alongside a half glimpsed, submerged slave boat; moorings
of logbooks stir in the archives: "Wednesday 20 May 1786 Buryed
a man slave (no. 34), Thursday . . . buried a boy slave (no. 86)." We,
too, bury our dead and forget their journeys through the city like talk
of almost suicide. The distance between daily routine and despair. In
87 years, he had gone from a bombed-out house in Langham Street
to the hillside of St Anthony's in that bright July of 1914.

On Sweeting Street Catherine read a phone message that asked:
"Did he mean to fail? Is he likely to do it again? Can we possibly
know—since we now have to pretend to know—what motivated
him?"

Glimpsing a child in a Galway street "a changeling," she thought.
The numbed semi-circle left by the surgeon's knife.

Are our lives determined by the times in which we live? "That's
real life," says Oisín as he blows smoke up through the blue
October sky. It is years since he saw his daughter. He stands up to
go back inside to collect a picture of her. "Oh sure, I have it here on

my phone. I'm such a luddite." My mind continues to follow him on the journey he does not take back to his office to collect the real live document, the actual photograph of his daughter. I remember sitting in this exact place hearing about her new pony, the death of her puppy, her trials and tribulations at school. He shows me a digital picture on his phone of a young woman: "She's fifteen there." The image is one he has found on the internet: "Her mother should send me news of her but she knows it hurts me to have the silence and so . . ." Six months talking to a shrink: "The time passes, you know."

On St Stephen's Green, Easter Monday 1916, James Stephens heard an Irish Volunteer say: "We have everything now."

"Could you be pregnant?" She answered a sentence where the words "immaculate" and "conception" fell and broke.

My story is broken twice by ghosts.

G. Daniels Ekarte who arrived into Liverpool in 1915 from Calabar kept a notebook of all the racist incidents that happened to him: "Then God entered into my soul. I throws the notebook into the River Mersey along with my gun. I had planned to go back to Africa and shoot the missionaries after making them read this book. They had lied to me."

WALKING

On Faulkner Road Jane recalled:
He said: "Have you heard the news?"
And I said I had. Now was he thinking:
"If I hadn't have recommended that John Lennon wouldn't make it
as an artist
he might still be alive today."
We never spoke about that.
We never spoke of that at all.
I just felt I could read what he was thinking.

On Elbow Lane Neema said:
The ship might not go out today. Too windy.
Be careful walking about the docks in this wind.
Bits fly about everywhere. Not safe.

On Oakhill Road Charlie said:
You're mother's eyes light up when she talks about her time at Tate's,
don't they Fri.

On Scotland Road Dave said:
They'd been locked out and I thought it would just be a one,
two-day affair...
I still remember it to this day—
I went down to the Elm House pub and I was greeted
by the sacked dockers as though I was a long-lost son
as though they'd known me all my life.

On Bracknel Avenue Lynn said:
Kirkby people stopped paying their rent because conditions were so bad...
There was almost a different sense of self with people from Kirkby.
They were moved out from Scotland Road
A mini republic within a republic.

16

1990: NELSON MANDELA FREED

I read the obituary of Liverpool's Lyceum building on Bold Street
in the National Library of Ireland where the documentary memory
of Europe's first lending library is kept:

Essay on Happiness to come 1755
Essay on the means of happiness 1755
Estlin's apology for the Sabbath 1801
Estlin's evidences of revealed religion 1796
Eumenes, dialogues of, 1719
Farmer's dissertations on miracles 1771
Capper's journey to India 1802
Carraccioli's travels of reason in Europe 1780
Carr's travels round the Baltic 1805
Chandler's travels through Asia Minor 1775
Chardin's travels into Persia 1686
Chastelleaux's travels in North America 1787
Corry's observations on the windward coast of Africa 1807
Cox's account of Russian discoveries 1778
Rules and regulations of the gaol at Gloucester 1790
St John's letters from an American farmer 1782
Sarratt on Chess 1808
Saunders on Theaters 1790
Second thoughts concerning the war 1755
Thoughts on the establishment of a Protestant nunnery 1809
Voltaire's Works, by Franklin 1762–81

Standing at the border Walter Benjamin said: "In 1932, when I was abroad, it began to be clear to me that I would soon have to bid a long, perhaps lasting farewell to the city of my birth . . . In this situation . . . I deliberately called to mind those images which, in exile, are most apt to waken homesickness: images of childhood. My assumption was that the feeling of longing would no more gain mastery over my spirit than a vaccine does over a healthy body."

I know they are here. Deep within a village of their lives. Like living in the middle of a deep forest. I know they are here in this city. They are here. Tonight.

A far-off voice. A bad line. A long impossible number to call that includes too many zeros and an official "eight." A name she didn't quite catch. Shirley, Shelly. Sounded with Lancashire or India in the acoustics of distance. Someone reading from a script, delivering a monologue without feeling or pause before reaching another script of questions answered less than twelve hours ago on a computer in the job centre on Williamson Square that smelt of anxiety and cigarettes. *This call will be recorded.*
Confirm your full name, date of birth, number of house, post code.
So many intimate questions as though shouted across a crowded silent room.
Have you suffered abuse by someone or by a family member in the past two weeks?
This may affect your "waiting time."
Do you need to take out a loan to tide you over?
Have you a dependent child even one that visits you once or more a week?
Have you a British passport?
Have you been out of the country for more than four weeks at a time over the past two years?
If you are late for your appointment tomorrow it will result in your claim being voided.

She stares down at the back of the garage doors on Roscoe Lane.
Clonmel.
Shoemaker.
The ancestors catch her searching for them through the attic window.
An Irish west coast lament of islanders mourn their losses; looking
out to sea I search the waters and the rocks; comb the beaches for
patterns knitted and shaped to the shoulders and waists of daughters,
sons, fathers, mothers, husbands, lovers, brothers, sisters, friends who
left and did not yet arrive.

Back in the library:
Lloyds register of shipping.
The Complete Letters of Henry James, 1884-1888.
Five Weeks in a Balloon, Jules Verne.
The newspaper stand is empty: "We are having a problem with
our supplier."
(A gap in the future archive)

In the museum next door, I see my reflection in a fragment of glass;
a mirror cut with sharp edges deep into the stomach of the Congo.

Walking along the Pier Head
a woman reads aloud words etched in a public monument
that looks out to the River Mersey:
To the Chinese Merchant Seamen who served this country well
during both world wars.
For those who gave their lives for this country.
For the many Chinese merchant seamen who after both world wars
were required to leave.
For their wives and partners who were left in ignorance
of what had happened to their men.
To the children who never knew their fathers.

On Eldonian Way Sister Mary Agnes laughing to herself remembered:
Visiting around Scotland Road
We went up into the high flats where Protestants lived
We have to go to everyone. That is our mission—to go to everyone;
Delivering leaflets with quotations from the Gospel,
nobody opened their door.
When we left
a shower of paper
came down on top of us.
The leaflets
all torn.

In the Liverpool Commercial Register *of 1780*
Captain Thomas Ralph said:
RUN AWAY, on the 18th of April last, from PRESCOT.
Aged twenty years, about five feet seven. Had on a green coat,
red waistcoat and blue breeches . . . speaks English pretty well.
Any person who will bring the black to the Talbot Inn,
in Liverpool, shall be handsomely rewarded.

17

2011: THE "ARAB SPRING"

A thread of amber
I stand on snow and find where due north places my life.
A river separating time into the valley.
I travel closer to the mountain, further from the city.

The rain is coming. The garden darkens. The clocks tick out the
measure of my time. I wait with Jean Guéhenno:

The German Army occupied France yesterday. The letter I receive each
Monday from my grandfather tells me he is alive.

I cannot write back—to tell him that I received his life line, that I am
thinking of him. The post is banned that way.

Radio Luxembourg. Éireann. I follow the dial of the radio and then
turn into St Anthony and the Sacred Heart. Searching for a Hindu
temple, I find an old Welsh chapel painted red.

Walking through the city like the last ghost, I see other last ghosts.
The Cunard Building. Empty passenger lounges and first-class
waiting rooms

waiting
for what?
Private telephone booths emptied of news, last minute dispatches,
conversations made by one class to their own.

The city rains night. Lights burning time out to the river and across to where the bombs fell. April already. Distances etched into this landscape of relationships like the gaping yields of a quarry. Over there. I know they are not two miles away.

A dark front of fallen life. Codes broken and long forgotten. A former Resistance fighter who served in the 1970s at the perfume counter in George Henry Lees held all the secrets of the city. "I was prepared to put my life on the line to do what we could. We all were."

I pass through Sweeting Street. Alderman Thomas Sweeting, Mayor of Liverpool in 1698. Elbow Lane. Another once-upon-a-time bank built by an émigré who founded the synagogue on Hope Place that is now the Unity Theatre where Catherine performing Brecht in 1988 said: "Acting and working / Learning and teaching / Intervene from your stage / In the Struggles of our Time. / Make the experience of struggle / the property of all / Transform justice / into a passion."

On the intricate journeys west into Galway, all the old arguments faded into wild-flowers of civility; further west we felt the sea in our dreams as we lay on that make-shift racecourse. The daughter's hair everywhere like seaweed, she thought. Golden red. A ponytail of spun gold. Connemara. A shared history of longing saturates their homecoming.

Something about time passing, children growing. Like coming out of a fever. Stumbling into the street with a suitcase.

This photograph of Liverpool is too much of the color of 1965. What would 1972 look like? Were people starting to feel less free? The Orange Lodge marching. 12 July 1972, what did this glance at Liverpool mean?

On Rodney Street in 1847 Dr. Duncan said:
The Irish poor inhabit the filthiest and worst
ventilated courts and cellars.

On Saltney Street a Donegal man working on the building site
of the Tobacco Warehouse said:
Steven Gerrard was up here recently.

On Coronation Drive Ada said:
I used to walk round the newly bombed sites with my father;
holding a mirror inside the rubble to see if there was breath.

On Brownlow Hill on 18th December 1847
the workhouse records said:
Aged 11, 9, 17, 23, 3, 3, 4, 62.
Gill, Gaskell, Griffin, Duffy.
Discharged: To the lunatic asylum
Released: From fever ward at own request.
Released: To the Industrial School.
Michael Higgins: Escaped over the wall.
Patrick Hagan: Died in boys' ward.

On Bent Street in November 1849 James Cassidy said:
"I am thirty years a porter but I have not earned a day's wages
for the last seven weeks."

18

2 JULY 2016: ANTI-BREXIT MARCH FOR EUROPE

What would you say if she asked?
The narrative was never clear in her mind.
And now it didn't matter.
And yet—
she still could not speak without collapsing through the years.
She had watched for too long
time fall apart.

The local geography of my parents' lives are etched into these
pavements, disappeared buildings, repetitive journeys from one
street to another; one shop and then home, from this school gate
to that church. From the larder to the sink. From the kitchen to
the hallway. The numbers of their ration books stay in their minds.
The numbers glimpsed on his arm. Mr. H, the egg man. The milk
in bottles delivered to the doorstep. The places at table. Her nana's
half-sister found walking up and down Paradise Street at five in the
morning looking for her father John Walsh who had died decades
before in another chapter of Ireland's faltering memory. The flat
where she lived looked derelict. Her mind had lost who we were
that Christmas morning: I was my daughter and I had fallen.

I mourn everything. The past is almost as absent as the future. Could
it have been different? I don't know. The structure of the unknown
streets always confused me. My parents' house begins to contract as
they, too, are made to leave home again.

At the Walker Art Gallery:
Two women
their bodies frozen in iced mid-air
Purgatory.
I look up at the picture that hangs above:
Cradled in a blanket and left on the edges of a field,
a shepherd found her.

"Do not let them take your child away from you."

Silenced and suspended in ice, I stayed for three decades.
Panes of glass, the passing streets, the quarried rock.

The former navigations across Liverpool had taken place in a fog.
The maps had been wrong.
At 8pm when he fell to the living room floor,
The city re-settled an inch or so out of focus.
The eighteenth-century sugar cone melted into tea.
"You would not know me I am so failed.
You would not know me . . ."

Catherine reading the part of Susan in Virginia Woolf's *The Waves*
as the sun left the chapel in Cambridge said to Emma:
"Then like a cracked bowl the fixity of my morning broke, and putting down
the bags of flour I thought, Life stands round me like a glass round the
imprisoned reed."

The Hunger Strikes left her grandmother without speech; when she
began to talk it took a priest from Africa to understand that what she
was not saying, she was not saying in Irish.

"Those moments in which a token of the future lies hidden."

The archives. A city's memory. Incriminating pro-confederate papers
quickly destroyed by Liverpool's ship, arms, engine builders.

On Great Homer Street a tour guide said:
There are Irish bodies all over the city
2,000 bodies found in a pit in St John's Garden.

In St John's Gardens Jess said:
Swallow, swallow, little swallow.
Won't you stay with me for one night longer.

On Stanley Road Francis said:
The total deaths in Liverpool in 1847 was 17, 280 70% of these were
Irish deaths.

On Abercromby Square Garstang wrote:
A Preliminary note on an expedition to Meroe in Ethiopia.

On Berkley Street Carissa said:
The Agios Nikolaos
Greek Orthodox Church
on the corner of Berkley Street and Princes Road in Toxteth,
golden-red
unframed effigies
kissed.
Very Irish. Men in one part; women in another.
Like a party in my mother's house.

On Parliament Street Nadezhda said:
A music working group with the Charles Wotton Centre
released an anti-apartheid record.

19

21 JANUARY 2017: WOMEN'S MARCH ON WASHINGTON

In *X-Ray Plath* on a staircase in Galway for Culture Night,
Third Voice said: "I wasn't ready. The white clouds rearing
Aside were dragging me in four directions.
I wasn't ready.
I had no reverence.
I thought I could deny the consequence—
But it was too late for that. It was too late, and the face
Went on shaping itself with love, as if I was ready."

In a newspaper in the library she read: "German researchers said
on Wednesday that they were launching an attempt to reassemble
millions of shredded East German secret police files using
complicated computerized algorithms."

At the dock-side entrance to the warehouse alongside Saltney Street
she saw Maud Gonne speaking at the anti-conscription open-air
rally. Concerts for the Gaelic League. 78 Duke Street their
headquarters. A glance away from the city's first public library, now
headquarters of Bibby's, the only shipping company still based in
the city.

*"But to return" Catherine said as Susan: "Let us again pretend that life is a
solid substance, shaped like a globe, which we turn about in our fingers. Let
us pretend that we can make out a plain and logical story—"*

"When are you going to stop all this?" the nuns had asked her.
"Are you going to read all of that book?" Her mother's sister enquired.

Of course, it was the question of abortion that always stopped the Spanish Civil War conversation somewhere between Lourdes and Thursday's Catholic Mothers' Union meetings. "Once a Catholic, always a Catholic." An answer given by her mother that confounded her: "*God* knows you believe, even if *you* don't."

Belfast in the 1980s was the closest frame of reference she had encountered to understanding the Liverpool her mother and ancestors had lived through. Between Netherfield Road and Scotland Road: "they stabbed the donkey pulling the cart with our belongings," her nana said as she described moving into a Protestant part of Liverpool in the middle of the 1926 General Strike. "They could tell I was a Catholic by the shape of my face."

Silence
"Where's da?"
"He can't speak to you."

" *'In this silence,' said Catherine reading the part of Susan 'it seems as if no leaf would ever fall, or bird fly.'* "

Moscow Drive, Russian Drive, Kremlin Drive. Belfast Road, Dublin Road. What does it mean to be *from* when the houses are boarded up into blackness? At number twelve Mrs Free's white Alice flowers pushed out through scuffed brickwork. Shadows where street signs had been.

She waits. King Street, New Market, Castle Street, Moon Street, Tea Brow, Dry Dock, Wett Dock, Salt Walk, Dale Street, Old Hall Street, Elm Street, Tythbarn Street, Blackberry Lane, Butchers Shambles.

On Princes Road a historic pamphlet said:
At the Synagogue we have seat rental accommodation
for 290 persons: 169 gentlemen and 121 ladies.

On Bold Street the News from Nowhere women's collective said:
Over in Whitechapel
We had loads of Fascist attacks.
All throughout the 80s. National Front.
We were set on fire a dozen times.
On Saturdays they'd come into the shop and knock
the bookshelves over and assault people. Break windows.

On Thomas Steers Dock, Gomer said:
From the first day of January 1806 to the first day of May 1807,
there had sailed from the port of Liverpool 185 African ships,
measuring 43,755 tons that were allowed to carry 49, 213 slaves.

In New Hall College, Corinna performing as Bernada Alba said:
What's this noise in my house amidst all this stifling silence?

On 8th December 1849 in Brownlow Hill Workhouse
Mary Percy, newly arrived from Ireland, screamed over and over:
What shall I do without my tongue?

25 MAY 2018: REPEAL THE 8TH

Which ancestor answered "Traveller" when asked about his father for a marriage certificate?

Catherine as Susan thinks: I am fenced in, planted here like one of my own trees. I say, "My son," I say, "My daughter."

At the Pier Head she looked out at a young woman arriving into the city from Dublin at midnight. The woman was searching across from the boat at a man. Her father. Waiting to collect her. Was the child with him? She could remember no more details. The deep quarry of Lime Street Station was another place she had lived. These points on the city's map of arrivals and departures, doorways, school gates. Carrying nothing. "Nothing will come of nothing. Speak again fool."

Mother: "But your nana was raised by her grandmother."
Daughter: "Yes, but her mother died when she was two.
I am not dead."

"What is that feeling? There, *that* feeling. Now?" Evelyn asks her in a city on the edge of Europe. She remembers Franz Fanon: "But the war goes on; and we will have to bind up for years to come the many, sometimes ineffaceable, wounds that the colonial onslaught has inflicted on our people."

A diary lay open in Saint Francis Xavier's, she read in the perfect handwriting of a priest: "Another bomb went off today in the shelter. Children late coming to class."

At a bus stop by Toxteth Workhouse (now Asda) she listens to Dickens as he passes inside to visit the Irish soldiers ill from their four month boat journey to Liverpool from Calcutta on the Great Tasmania: "It was raining hard when they put him in the open cart to bring him here, and he had the presence of mind to ask to have a sovereign taken out of his pocket that he had there, and a cab engaged, probably it saved his life. The patient rattled out the skeleton of a laugh, and said, proud of the story, 'Deed surr an open cart was a comical means o bringin a dying man here, and a clever way to kill him.'"

In St James' cemetery she read the stone inscriptions of those who belonged to each other: Catherine Widow of the above; Son of, daughter of, wife of. Names, places where they were born or lived or died. Dates and names inscribed in stone: two hundred years later, where they were from and to whom they belonged was still declared and known in the elements of a late afternoon stroll.

In her nana's tin-box a letter from her ancestor Mary Quinn dated February 1887 from Corbally, Dromore in County Tyrone to her son Michael in Victoria Gardens, Liverpool is saturated with grief: "Dear Mick, the news around here is not much only times is dull I would wish you would write often to me for I will not be long on this way would I fear my day is drawing near am very feeble only able to walk through the house . . . Soon I will be mingling with the angels in heaven. I can assure you that we cannot find words to express our heartfelt sorrow for your sad loss of your kind good wife may the almighty god have mercy on her soul . . ."

. . . the slow pendulum seen through the letter box of a porch.

Atmospheres are like tarot cards or leaves at the bottom of a tea cup. To *read* an atmosphere you have to forget the bruises on her eyes and look closely at the way the lines on my hand cut into each other or swerve off into 1889 and that song Jack Yeats heard in Sligo. The once fostered child sat close to the fire. She watched them from a distance through a doorway in the hall. He had found his way back; not unlike the Hungarian student after the revolution. Just like him; mistaking charity for love. They will never come this way again, she thought: another Irish fairy-tale forgotten in the telling.

When I think about the structure of their living architecture, I can see that they lived all their lives in the house where they were born . . . as my mother grew into their mother, the women collectively closed the gap on distance.

Where are you now?
Are you working?
So what are you doing?
Are you on your own?

Her questions were always the same. "Where are you?" My mother was so confused the last time we spoke by the vagueness of my answers—all of which were spoken to an impossible truth—that she asked: "But where are you right at this minute so I can picture exactly where you are?"

ILLUSTRATIONS

Prologue
Bruno Ganz and Otto Sander in *Wings of Desire* by Wim Wenders
© 1987 Road Movies—Argos Films
Courtesy of Wim Wenders Stiftung—Argos Films

1

Still from Liverpool Scenes (Lumière Brothers, 1896). St George's Hall
and (now demolished) St John's Church is in the background; a cart
delivers milk to the station; a boy walks across the road looking directly
into the camera. Courtesy of the BFI National Archive

2

Ships dock at the newly built Pier Head Liver Buildings, 1912

3

Unemployed March from Liverpool to London, May Day. Courtesy of
Merseyside Museum of Labour History

4

The only piece of stained glass in the depicting Liverpool's trade with the
British Empire that was not destroyed during World War II

5

Family evicted from home in Donegal 1888. Photography by Robert
French. Courtesy of the National Library of Ireland
(Call Number: L_IMP_1507)

6

Court housing, Johnson Street, Liverpool, 1935

7

Author's mother and her fellow Tate & Lyle women workers gather for a photograph outside the Liverpool sugar factory, c. 1950. Courtesy of the Liverpool Central Library

8

Irish Travellers. Photograph taken by Richard Tilbrook in June 1963. Courtesy of the National Library of Ireland (Call Number: TIL 859).

9

Textile token left by a mother who placed her baby in the Foundling Hospital. Women left matching token such as this with the baby so that, if they were ever in a position to reclaim them, they had some way of proving that the child was theirs

10

The Mujeras Libres, the Free Women, anarchist revolutionary group formed during the Spanish Civil War

11

Photograph taken by Richard Eastham of child sleeping, Mann Island at the Albert Docks Liverpool 11 August 1908. Courtesy of the Liverpool Central Library

12

Women Street Cleaners at the bottom of Hunter Street, Liverpool, 21 March 1916

13

The Tate & Lyle Sugar Silo is a Grade II listed building on Regent Road at Huskisson Dock in Kirkdale, north Liverpool. Henry Tate established his Liverpool refinery in 1872, and Tate & Lyle built their huge concrete sugar silo. The author's father was one of the workers on this construction site in the 1950s

14

An anchor stone carving on a sailor's gravestone, St James' Cemetery, Liverpool, 1840

15

Liverpool-born Trade Union leader Jim Larkin speaking at the 1913 Dublin Lock Out: "The great only appear great because we are on our knees. Let us rise"

16

National Library of Ireland, 1995. Courtesy of Tim Maul

17

Orange Lodge Marching, Lime Street, Liverpool, 1965

18

Photograph by Richard Eastham of two braille readers leaving the Central Library in 1915. Courtesy of the Liverpool Central Library

19

Woman worker selling potatoes at Liverpool's Albert Dock, c. 1898

20

Giovanni Segantini, *The Punishment of Lust,* 1891. Oil on canvas. Walker Art Gallery, Liverpool

ACKNOWLEDGMENTS

I thank all who generously took time to walk with me sharing insights and stories of the self and the city. I am thankful also to Arts Council England and to the remarkable librarians and archivists at Central Library Liverpool for enabling the beginnings of my writing and research as an artist practice. Thanks to friends, colleagues and students from around the world and to those who engaged so thoughtfully with drafts of my artist project over the years. I am very grateful to Klaus Ottmann for his insightful and artistic curation of this book. I write my special thanks in memory of my mother and father and with love always to my daughter.